My Amazing Toddler Behavioral Series

I Do Not Give Up. I Learn From Mistakes!

By Suzanne T. Christian

TWO**RAVENS**
B O O K S

Two Little Ravens
CHILDREN'S NON-FICTION BOOKS

Paperback Edition: 9781964202051
Hardcover Edition: 9781964202068
Digital Edition: 9781964202075

Published in the United States by Two Ravens Books LLC,
254 Chapman Rd, Ste 209, Newark DE 19702

'Expand the mind, free the imagination, one title at a time.'
www.tworavensbooks.com

Welcome to
I Do Not Give Up.
I Learn From Mistakes!

This book is a delightful collection of simple affirmations designed specifically for young children. As you explore its pages together, your child will learn the importance of resilience, patience, and the courage to try again.

Each page features vibrant illustrations and relatable scenarios, encouraging a positive attitude toward making mistakes. By making this book a regular part of your reading routine, you empower your toddler to develop a strong foundation of confidence and perseverance, as repetition is a proven teaching tool.

Prepare for a journey of growth, learning, and lots of fun with your toddler!

Suzanne T. Christian

Mistakes are just part of my adventure!

Oops! I can fix that
and make it right.

Every time I learn,
I grow big and strong.

If I fall,
I get back up
and try again!

When I make mistakes, I find new ways to do it better.

It's fun to keep trying,
even when it's hard!

Mistakes are how I learn new things every day.

I love trying new things because I'm not afraid to learn.

If I don't get it right,
I can try again.

Coloring outside the lines just means I'm making art my way!

When my block
tower tumbles down,
I laugh and build it
back up again!

I never give up
because I am brave.

When I put my shoe
on the wrong foot,
I giggle and switch
it around!

Every try makes
me smarter!

I keep going,
even when it's hard.
I do not give up!

Oops! That didn't work,
but I can find a new way!

Learning new
things is like
a game, and
I love to play!

Every mistake
helps me grow.

When I try and try,
I get better and better!

Oops!
I made a mess,
but I can clean
it up.

I smile when
I try again.

I do not give up!
I learn from
mistakes
The End!

My Amazing Toddler Behavioral Series

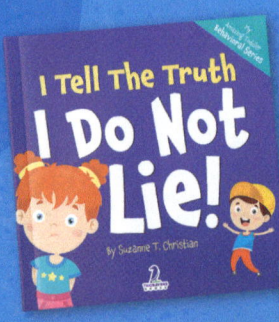

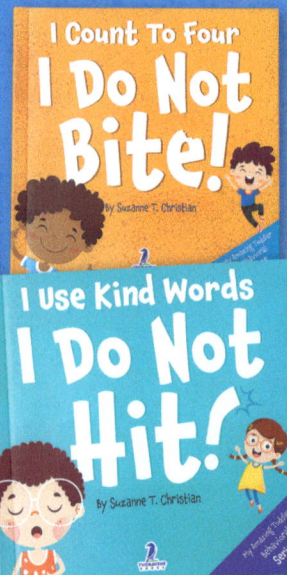

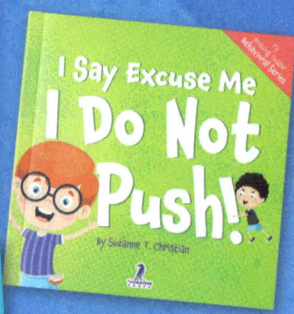

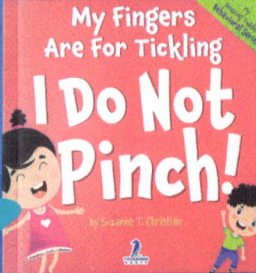

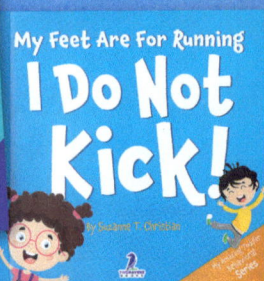

Check Out
Suzanne T. Christian's beloved series
'My Amazing Toddler Behavioral Series'.
Young readers are sure to enjoy!

Two Little Ravens
CHILDREN'S NON-FICTION BOOKS

Dear Amazing Reader,

Thank you for diving into **I Do Not Give Up! I Learn From Mistakes!** with me. If this book touched your heart or made a difference for a young reader, I'd be grateful if you could share your thoughts in a review. Your feedback inspires my future work and helps others discover the magic within these pages.

I'd love to hear from you directly if you have suggestions or ideas for improving the book. Please feel free to reach out to me at **suzanne.christian@tworavensbooks.com.** Your voice counts, and I cherish it deeply.

With heartfelt gratitude,

www.ingramcontent.com/pod-product-compliance
Lightning Source LLC
Chambersburg PA
CBHW041559120626
46551CB00002B/263

9781964202051